Key Stage 3

Philosophy and Ethics

Robert Orme

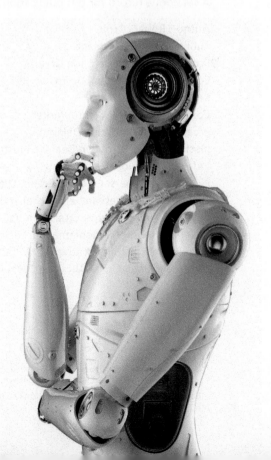

William Collins' dream of knowledge for all began with the publication of his first book in 1819. A self-educated mill worker, he not only enriched millions of lives, but also founded a flourishing publishing house. Today, staying true to this spirit, Collins books are packed with inspiration, innovation and practical expertise. They place you at the centre of a world of possibility and give you exactly what you need to explore it.

Collins. Freedom to teach.

Published by Collins
An imprint of HarperCollins*Publishers*
The News Building
1 London Bridge Street
London
SE1 9GF

HarperCollins *Publishers*
1st Floor
Watermarque Building
Ringsend Road
Dublin 4
Ireland

Browse the complete Collins catalogue at
www.collins.co.uk

Text © Robert Orme 2019
Design © HarperCollins*Publishers* Limited 2019

10 9 8 7

ISBN 978-0-00-835502-9

Robert Orme asserts his moral right to be identified as the author of this work.

British Library Cataloguing-in-Publication Data
A catalogue record for this publication is available from the British Library.

Author: Robert Orme
Publisher: Katie Sergeant
Product manager: Caroline Green
Editorial assistant: Simone Taylor
Reviewer: Neil McKain
Copyeditor: Hugh Hillyard-Parker
Proof reader: Catherine Dakin
Illustrator: Nigel Dobbyn/Beehive Illustration
Indexer: Lisa Footitt
Picture researchers: Caroline Green, Simone Taylor and Tina Pietron
Text permissions researcher: Rachel Thorne
Cover and internal typesetter: Ken Vail Graphic Design
Cover photograph: Phonlamai Photo/Shutterstock
Production controller: Katherine Willard
Printed and Bound in the UK using 100% Renewable Electricity at CPI Group (UK) Ltd

MIX
Paper from
responsible sources
FSC™ C007454

Contents

Introduction

Philosophers ask questions, often very difficult questions. What is reality? How can we know what is true? Is there a god? What makes us human? How should we live?

Philosophers have been trying to answer these questions for millennia. Some 2500 years ago, an Ancient Greek man named Socrates wandered the streets of Athens questioning the ideas of people around him, challenging them to justify their beliefs. Socrates is often thought to be one of the first philosophers in the Western world. His constant questioning of everything caused such concern to the Greek authorities that they forced him to drink poison, which killed him. However, Socrates had started something. Another Ancient Greek philosopher Plato and his student Aristotle carried on questioning the ideas of those around them. This questioning has continued over the past 2500 years.

In this book, you will explore some of the most interesting and influential ideas that humans have ever thought. You will meet a wide range of philosophers whose contributions to Western thought lead many to think of them as some of the greatest minds to ever live. Some you might agree with; others you might think are entirely wrong. That is all part of philosophy: listening, thinking, questioning and debating ideas, working out whether or not you think they work and why that is. I hope it is a journey that you find interesting and rewarding.

Robert Orme

Concise topic introductions set the scene for each topic.

Photographs and artwork help to illustrate and embed key concepts.

Fact boxes provide interesting, bite-sized information.

Check your understanding questions at the end of every topic allow you to check and consolidate your learning.

Key vocabulary lists (in alphabetical order) at the end of each unit help you to find and define important terminology.

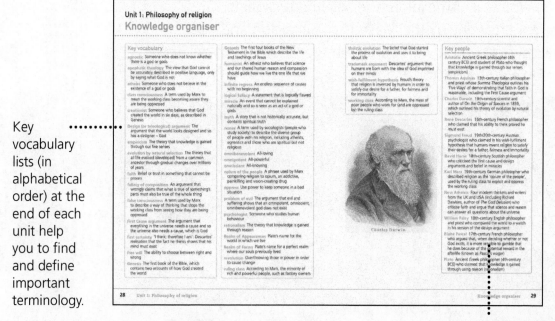

Key people lists (in alphabetical order) recap the people of influence covered in each unit.

Philosophy of religion

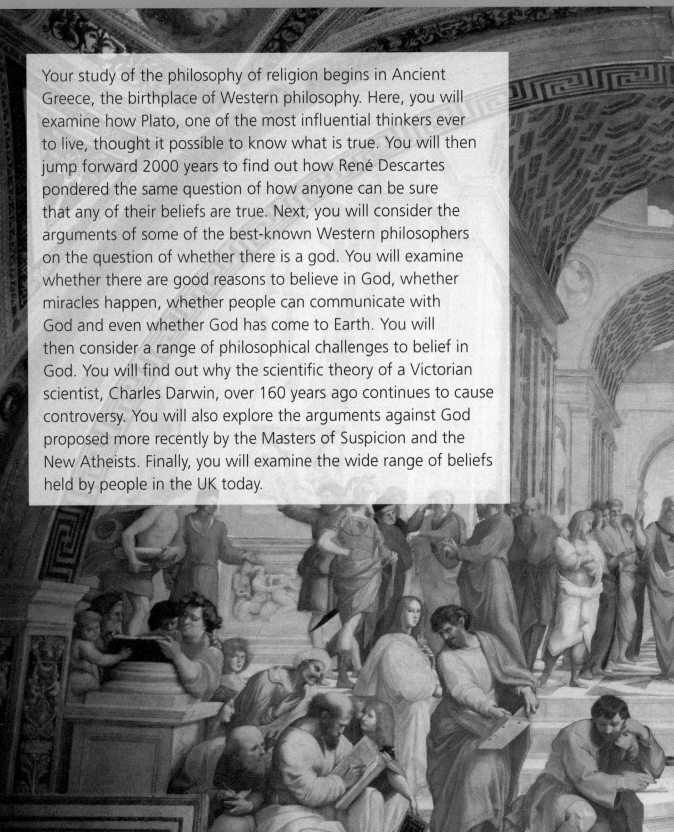

Your study of the philosophy of religion begins in Ancient Greece, the birthplace of Western philosophy. Here, you will examine how Plato, one of the most influential thinkers ever to live, thought it possible to know what is true. You will then jump forward 2000 years to find out how René Descartes pondered the same question of how anyone can be sure that any of their beliefs are true. Next, you will consider the arguments of some of the best-known Western philosophers on the question of whether there is a god. You will examine whether there are good reasons to believe in God, whether miracles happen, whether people can communicate with God and even whether God has come to Earth. You will then consider a range of philosophical challenges to belief in God. You will find out why the scientific theory of a Victorian scientist, Charles Darwin, over 160 years ago continues to cause controversy. You will also explore the arguments against God proposed more recently by the Masters of Suspicion and the New Atheists. Finally, you will examine the wide range of beliefs held by people in the UK today.

Unit 1: Philosophy of religion
How did Plato think we can know the truth?

Why did Plato think that our senses cannot tell us what is real?

Western philosophy began approximately 2500 years ago in Ancient Greece. Two of the earliest and most influential Ancient Greek philosophers were **Plato** and **Aristotle**. Plato observed that everything in the world was constantly changing. For example, things age, change temperature, size and shape. Nothing in the world that we can see, smell, taste, touch or hear stays the same. Therefore, the moment we think we have understood something, it has changed and so is no longer the same thing. This led Plato to conclude that we cannot rely on our five senses to give us accurate information about reality. It is only possible to gain true knowledge by using our minds, or reason alone, to reflect on unchanging things. Plato believed these unchanging things exist in another realm.

The Realm of Forms

Plato thought there are two different parts to a human: a physical body and a non-physical, immortal soul. He argued that before the soul joined the body, it lived in another realm called the **Realm of Forms**. In the Realm of Forms, there is a perfect, unchanging 'form' of the things that can be seen in the world around us. For example, goodness, honesty and beauty exist in their perfect, unchanging form. It is unclear whether Plato thought that there is a perfect form of every quality and object in the Realm of Forms – for example, a perfect form of badness, jealousy, apple, tree, insect and so on – or whether he thought that there were only perfect forms of some qualities, such as goodness.

The Realm of Appearances

Plato called the world in which we live the **Realm of Appearances**. He claimed everything in the Realm of Appearances is merely a reflection or shadow of its real, true form. He believed that when we see something in the world, such as beauty, we recognise that it is similar to the perfect form of beauty that our soul experienced in the Realm of Forms. However, everything that we see in this world is simply an imperfect, shadowy copy of its true form. For example, if we were to zoom in closely, we would realise that every circle we have ever seen is an imperfect circle. However, we still recognise the shapes as circles because they are similar to the perfect form of circle. Likewise, we have never experienced a perfect act of kindness, but we call things 'kind' because they resemble the perfect form of kindness.

Think

Think of three things you know for certain. Can you prove for certain that these things are true? How?

How does an apple constantly change? What about a non-living thing, like a table?

The analogy of the cave

To illustrate his theory, Plato told a story called *the analogy of the cave*. He asks us to imagine prisoners who have spent their entire lives in an underground cave. They sit in front of a small wall, behind which is a fire that provides light. Every day, people walk past the wall carrying various objects. The prisoners cannot see the fire, the people or the objects. They can only see the shadows of the different objects reflected onto the cave wall they are facing. However, the prisoners think that the shadows are the actual objects; they do not realise they are shadows. Plato thought that people who trust their five senses to give them knowledge of the world are like the prisoners who think they are seeing reality, but are only seeing shadows or reflections of it.

Plato used the analogy of the cave to explain his ideas about human knowledge.

Many have criticised Plato's belief in the Realm of Forms because he provided no evidence of its existence. One critic was Plato's student Aristotle, who attended a school of philosophy set up by Plato in Athens. Aristotle disagreed with Plato that we can only understand reality by using reason. He did not believe in the Realm of Forms or that humans have a soul that is separate to our body. According to Aristotle, there is no reason to doubt that the things we see are real, and so we should use our five senses to understand reality.

Aristotle is known as an empiricist because he believed that we gain knowledge through our senses (**empiricism**). Plato was a rationalist meaning he believed that knowledge is gained through using our reason (**rationalism**). Today, most people believe that both rationalism and empiricism are helpful in understanding different things.

Raphael's painting *The School of Athens* portrays these two differing views. Plato is pointing up to show that we gain knowledge by using reason to reflect on the Realm of Forms. Aristotle is indicating towards the Earth to show that we gain knowledge by using our senses and the world around us.

Key vocabulary

empiricism The theory that knowledge is gained through our five senses

rationalism The theory that knowledge is gained through reason

Realm of Appearances Plato's name for the world in which we live

Realm of Forms Plato's name for a perfect realm where our souls previously lived

Check your understanding

1 Why did Plato claim that we cannot rely on our senses to understand reality?
2 Explain what Plato believed about the Realm of Appearances and the Realm of Forms.
3 Explain what happens in Plato's analogy of the cave.
4 What message is Plato trying to communicate through the analogy?
5 How were Aristotle's views different from those of Plato?

Unit 1: Philosophy of religion

Why did Descartes doubt everything?

How did Descartes think we can know what is true?

Are our senses deceiving us?

Think of something that you know is definitely true. How can you be certain? This was the question that troubled the 17th-century Christian philosopher, **René Descartes**. How can we be sure that anything that we _think_ is real and true actually _is_ real and true and not an illusion?

To solve this problem, Descartes decided that he would doubt everything that he believed; he would then see whether there was anything left at the end that he could know for certain. If he could not be 100 per cent certain about a belief, it would fail his test. Descartes decided that he could not trust his senses to tell him what is true because sometimes our senses give us false information. For example, when a drinking straw is put in water it looks bent, but this is not really the case. Sometimes we also think we have seen or heard something, but haven't. Therefore, Descartes ruled out the possibility of knowing anything for certain through empiricism (senses).

French philosopher René Descartes (1596–1650)

Are our minds being tricked?

Descartes also ruled out knowing anything for certain through rationalism (reason), for example mathematical truths such as 2 + 2 = 4. He thought that he could not prove that there is not an evil demon tricking us into thinking 2 + 2 = 4 every time we do the sum when actually 2 + 2 = 5! Descartes was troubled by the fact that everything his mind thought was real and true could be an illusion – he could be nothing more than a mind trapped in an evil demon's laboratory. If this were the case, Descartes wondered, what one thing could the demon _not_ trick his mind about?

Descartes realised that the demon would not be able to trick his mind into thinking it existed if it did not. In order for the demon to trick his mind, he would have to have a mind. He summed up this idea by writing one of the best-known lines in all of philosophy: 'I think; therefore I am.'

The first certainty

Descartes thought that the fact he could doubt his own existence meant he must exist. He did not think this proved he had a body; the demon could be tricking him into thinking he had a body. However, he must have a thinking mind; otherwise there would be nothing for the demon to trick.

Descartes did not think that this could prove that anybody else existed; these could still be illusions. It wouldn't work for him to say, 'You think; therefore you are' or 'We think; therefore we are', but he could be certain of his own existence. This is sometimes called the **first certainty** and is often written in Latin, _cogito ergo sum_.

Is the idea of God tattooed on our minds?

Although Descartes had managed to find one thing of which he could be certain, he wasn't satisfied with stopping there. In order to add further certainties, Descartes claimed that the idea of God is imprinted on our minds: in other words, people are born with an understanding of God. This is known as the **trademark argument**. Descartes thought that we have an inbuilt knowledge that God is 'the sum of all perfections'. By this, Descartes meant that God possesses every perfect characteristic – for example, God is completely loving, powerful and wise. Descartes also thought that in order for God to be perfect, he must exist. This is because things that exist in reality are better than things that only exist in our minds. For example, having one million pounds is better than the idea of having one million pounds. Existence is a perfection, so if God is the 'sum of all perfections', then he must exist.

The existence of a perfect God was important for Descartes because he thought that if a perfect God exists, God would not let his senses and mind be deceived. Therefore, Descartes concluded that he could trust that his mind and senses were giving him accurate knowledge about the world most of the time.

Was Descartes right?

Many people would disagree with Descartes that all humans are born with the idea of God imprinted on their minds. If everybody were born knowing what God is, then everybody would believe in the same God. However, through history, people have had very different ideas about what God is like. They have also disagreed about whether there is one god, many gods or no gods at all.

Secondly, many people would question Descartes' claim that things that exist in reality are better than things that exist in the imagination. For example, sometimes the idea of eating a delicious food can be better than actually eating it.

Furthermore, Descartes argues that God exists because in order for God to be perfect, God must exist. However, he does not begin by proving that there *is* a perfect god; he simply states that this is the case because he has been born with the idea of a perfect god imprinted on his mind.

I think, therefore I am. In other words, the fact that I am thinking shows that I exist. (the first certainty)

I will doubt absolutely everything.

The idea of God is imprinted on my mind; it is innate. (the trademark argument)

God is the 'sum of all perfections'.

If God is perfect, he must exist.

A perfect god would not allow us to be deceived. Therefore, we can generally trust our reason and experience to be accurate.

Descartes' thought journey

Key vocabulary

first certainty 'I think; therefore I am': Descartes' realisation that the fact he thinks shows that his mind must exist

trademark argument Descartes' argument that humans are born with the idea of God imprinted on their minds

Check your understanding

1 Why did Descartes decide to doubt everything?

2 Why did Descartes initially rule out knowing things through empiricism and rationalism?

3 What did Descartes mean by the phrase, 'I think; therefore I am'?

4 How did Descartes think that the idea of God made it possible to know things for certain?

5 Why might Descartes' view be criticised?

Unit 1: Philosophy of religion

Was God the first cause of everything?

Does the existence of our universe provide evidence that God exists?

Summa Theologica

Over the course of history, religious philosophers have developed arguments that aim to show that it is reasonable to believe in God. For example, the 13th-century Italian philosopher, **Thomas Aquinas** wrote a 4000-page, unfinished work about God called *Summa Theologica*. The two most famous pages explain his 'Five Ways' – five attempts to demonstrate that it is reasonable to believe in God. His Third Way is known as the **First Cause argument**.

The First Cause argument

Aquinas noticed that everything that exists relies on something else for it to begin existing; it is impossible for something to cause itself to exist because this would require it to exist before it existed! Aquinas did not think it logical to believe there had been an **infinite regress** (endless causes). He thought that something must have been a first cause and so he argued that there must be a skilful, powerful being who was the first cause of everything else. This is known as the First Cause argument. In short, the argument is:

1. Everything in the universe has a cause.

2. If everything in the universe has a cause, the universe itself must have a cause.

3. The cause of the universe must be God.

Does the argument prove anything?

Some people think that Aquinas contradicts himself by arguing that everything needs a cause, whereas God does not. In response, it could be argued that God is outside the universe he created, and so he does not need a cause like everything in it. He is eternal.

Secondly, Aquinas assumes that an infinite regress is impossible, but this might not be the case. Even though it is hard for us to imagine, maybe there is an endless sequence of causes that goes back forever, meaning there was no beginning.

Thirdly, even if Aquinas was right that there was a first cause, it could be any kind of being or force, not necessarily the Christian God. Many scientists would argue that the Big Bang caused the universe. In response, a Christian could argue that God caused the Big Bang.

Thomas Aquinas (1225–1274) was one of the most influential theologians and philosophers ever to have lived.

Fact

Towards the end of his life, Aquinas concluded that everything he had written about God was like 'straw' because God is a mystery that cannot be fully understood by human minds.

To topple all the dominoes, something must make the first domino fall. In the same way, the First Cause argument claims that there must have been a first cause of the universe.

The fallacy of composition

The 18th-century Scottish philosopher, **David Hume**, was one of the first people to challenge religious belief. He claimed that the First Cause argument was based on a **logical fallacy** called the **fallacy of composition**. This fallacy is when one claims that what is true of something's parts must be true of the whole. For example, just because every player in a football team is good, that does not mean the team is good. In the same way, just because everything in the universe needs a cause, that does not mean the universe itself needs a cause.

The Design argument

In his Fifth Way, Aquinas argued that natural things in the world appear to have been designed and that this shows that there is an intelligent designer: God. This is known as the **Design (or teleological) argument** and can be summarised as follows:

1. The world around us looks as if it has been designed.

2. Designed things need an intelligent designer.

3. The intelligent designer of the world is God.

Inspired by Aquinas's original idea, an 18th-century English philosopher and priest called **William Paley** used the example of a watch in his version of the Design argument. He noted that all the complex parts of a watch fit together in an orderly way so that it can achieve its purpose of telling the time. This is not simply an accident that has happened by chance; it is because a watch has a watchmaker. Just as a watch needs a watchmaker, he argued, then something even more complex, orderly and purposeful like the world must have a world maker.

Does the argument prove anything?

The Design argument has been criticised for many reasons. Hume argued that the designer could be any sort of being or beings. Others have argued that the evil and suffering in the world are evidence of a bad designer not a perfect, god-like designer.

Perhaps the greatest challenge to the Design argument is **Charles Darwin's** theory of evolution by natural selection (see Topic 1.5) because it provides another explanation for why things look designed. Living things have adapted over millions of years, becoming more complex in order to survive. If they had not adapted and become complex, they would have died out. In response, it could be argued, if evolution is a blind, unconscious process, without anyone guiding it, it would be unlikely to result in something as complex as a human. Therefore, some would argue that perhaps God uses the method of evolution to create complex forms of life.

Paley compared the world to an intricately designed watch.

Key vocabulary

Design (or teleological) argument The argument that the world looks designed and so has a designer – God

fallacy of composition An argument that wrongly claims that what is true of something's parts must also be true of the whole thing

First Cause argument The argument that everything in the universe needs a cause and so the universe also needs a cause – God

infinite regress An endless sequence of causes with no beginning

logical fallacy A statement that is logically flawed

Check your understanding

1. Who was Thomas Aquinas and what did he write?

2. Explain the First Cause argument.

3. With reference to Hume, explain why the First Cause argument might be criticised.

4. Explain the Design argument and why it might be criticised.

5. 'The existence of our complex universe makes it likely that there is a god.' Discuss.

Unit 1: Philosophy of religion
Is God involved in the world?

Do religious experiences provide evidence that God exists?

Do people experience God?

One reason people might believe in a god or higher power is because they believe they have experienced something supernatural. For example, they might claim that they have seen an angel, that God has spoken to them or that they have experienced a **miracle**, such as being healed of an illness. These experiences can cause a person to believe in God or strengthen their existing religious belief.

However, religious experiences do not provide such convincing evidence for those who have not had the experience. They are required to trust that the person claiming to have had a religious experience is not lying for some reason – for example, to achieve fame, earn money or persuade others that their religion is true. Even if someone believes that they are telling the truth about their experience, it is possible that they have misinterpreted what happened. This might be especially likely when they are tired, grieving, fasting or under the influence of drugs.

Does God answer prayers?

Another reason people might believe in God is that they feel a sense of God's closeness or presence when they pray. They may also believe that some of their prayers have been answered. However, others would argue many prayers appear _not_ to be answered. It would seem random for some prayers to be answered while others are not. Doubters would say that it is more likely to be just a coincidence when prayers appear to be answered.

In response, a religious person might argue that there could be good reasons why God would not answer some prayers. Some prayers might be selfish or logically impossible to answer. For example, if two people prayed for their team to win a football match, it would not be possible for God to grant both requests. God's plan might be different from what people want and he might be doing what is best for people by _not_ giving them what they ask for.

Some people argue that claiming that we cannot understand why God acts in the way that he does is making an excuse for God rather than providing a good reason. Others argue that it is reasonable to think that some things, such as the activity of God, are beyond human understanding.

Prayer is an important part of many religions.

Has anybody seen God?

Sometimes people say that the only thing that would make them believe in God is if they saw him. Christians believe that, 2000 years ago, people living in the Middle East did see God because he came to Earth in the person of Jesus and lived among them. His life is written about in four books found in the Bible called the Gospels.

The Four Gospels

The **Gospels** are the first four books of the New Testament. They describe the life and teachings of Jesus and are named after the four men traditionally thought to have written them: Matthew, Mark, Luke and John. In the Gospels, Jesus speaks and acts as if he was God; for example, he forgives people for their sins, talks about what heaven is like and performs over 35 miracles, such as turning water to wine, walking on water, healing ill people and coming back to life after he is killed. In the books in the Bible that come after the Gospels, the authors claim that Jesus was God on Earth.

In the Gospel of Matthew, Jesus is said to have walked on water.

Most historians agree that a man named Jesus lived and that he was killed on a cross. However, there is much disagreement about whether the Gospels are a reliable source of information. They were written approximately 1900 years ago, and we do not have any certain information about their authors. It is possible that, after Jesus' death, people exaggerated what he had said and done in order to persuade others that he was God. Therefore, many people would say that there is not strong enough evidence to believe that Jesus was God on Earth.

Christians might respond by saying that they have experienced Jesus in their life, perhaps through prayer, a miracle or having a sense of him. They might argue that the brilliance of his teachings recorded in the Gospels shows that he was not just an ordinary person. Furthermore, Jesus is arguably the most influential person ever to have lived, with nearly one in three people in the world today following the religion that worships him – Christianity. A Christian might argue that it is unlikely that so many people can be completely wrong.

Jesus is arguably the most influential person ever to have lived.

Key vocabulary

Gospels The first four books of the New Testament in the Bible, which describe the life and teachings of Jesus

miracle An event that cannot be explained naturally and so is seen as an act of a god or gods

Check your understanding

1. Explain why David Hume was critical of belief in miracles.
2. Do you think religious experiences provide convincing evidence that God exists?
3. Why might a Christian argue that Jesus was God?
4. Why might it be argued that Jesus does not provide strong evidence for God's existence?
5. 'Unanswered prayers show that God probably does not exist.' Discuss.

Unit 1: Philosophy of religion
Can you believe in God and evolution?

Why did Darwin's theory about the origins of human life cause such a commotion?

On the Origin of Species

In 1859, a Victorian scientist called Charles Darwin wrote a book that changed the way people viewed life on Earth. It was called *On the Origin of Species.* Darwin explained that over millions of years, all life had evolved (developed) from a common ancestor: a single cell. After a very long time, through many gradual changes, humans had slowly developed or evolved from monkey-like creatures.

Darwin's theory is known as **evolution by natural selection.** Scientists accept Darwin's theory because of the evidence that supports it. For example, fossils show life developing from simple forms to more complex beings, and there is similarity between the DNA of living things, showing that they have a common ancestor. However, from the moment Darwin's book was published, it caused controversy.

Creationism: Genesis vs evolution

Many Christians in Victorian times interpreted the Bible literally. This meant that they believed that God had created all life in six days, as recorded in Chapter 1 of **Genesis**. The theory of evolution seemed to contradict Genesis, which suggests that creatures existed at the beginning of the world exactly as they do today. Furthermore, Victorian Christians thought that humans were the best part of God's creation, saved until last and made 'in God's image' on the final (sixth) day, once the world had been made ready for them. However, Darwin's theory suggested that there was nothing special about humans; they were just like every other animal that had to adapt to the world in order to survive. Some Christians today still reject the theory of evolution and believe that God created everything in six days. They are called **creationists.**

Darwin's book was published in 1859

Charles Darwin (1809–1882)

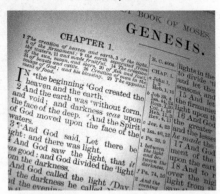
The book of Genesis, chapter 1

Fact

More than 98 per cent of our DNA is the same as chimpanzees and approximately 60 per cent is the same as chickens and bananas.

Finding fossils

Philip Gosse, a 19th-century creationist, claimed that fossils had been put in the ground by God to test whether people would abandon the truth of Genesis and follow science.

Day 1	Day 2	Day 3	Day 4	Day 5	Day 6	Day 7
Light and dark, day and night	Sky and seas	Land and plants	Sun, moon and stars	Birds and sea creatures	Animals and humans	God rests

The order of creation in Genesis 1

What is a *yom*?

Some Christians accept evolution, but still read Genesis literally. They point out that the Hebrew word for day in the Bible (*yom*) means a 'period of time'. Therefore, the 'days' in Genesis could be long periods of time, perhaps billions of years, where life developed through evolution. They might note that Genesis 1 and the theory of evolution put most things in the same order, with simple forms of life existing before more complex creatures.

Continuing controversy

Evolution remains controversial today. In some parts of the USA where creationism is popular, it is illegal to teach the theory of evolution in schools. In contrast, in the UK, schools can have their funding from the government withdrawn if they teach creationism as a scientific fact. In 2013, newspapers reported on an Orthodox Jewish school in North London that had crossed out questions on evolution from the GCSE science exam taken in their school.

Is Genesis a myth?

One problem with a literal interpretation of Genesis 1 is that light is created before the sun. Furthermore, in Genesis 2 there is a second version of the creation story where things are created in a different order. In Genesis 1, Adam and Eve are made together after the plants, but in Genesis 2, Adam was made before any plants appeared.

Many Christians think that where there are contradictions in the Bible, it is a sign that people should look for the deeper spiritual meaning rather than reading it as a historical or scientific account. They would say that Genesis is a **myth** revealing complex *spiritual truths* about reality, for example that God is the creative intelligence behind all that exists. They might argue that reading Genesis as a historical or scientific account of what happened on each day is missing the point. It would be like reading a poem or love letter that says 'your eyes are lakes' and thinking that the person has two large areas of water on their face, rather than understanding the writer's deeper message.

Christians who think that Genesis is a myth would say that both evolution and Genesis are right. Evolution explains *how* life was created whereas religion explains *why*. The name given to the belief that God started the process of evolution and uses it to bring about life is **theistic evolution**. After over a century of debate, the Catholic Church accepted this view in 1996. In a letter to a friend, Darwin wrote that he thought it 'absurd' to think that someone cannot believe in both God and evolution. However, others argue that there is no need for a god to be guiding the process of evolution in order for it to work. The theory can explain how life developed and why living things are so complex and well-suited to their environment, without the need for a god.

Key vocabulary

creationist Someone who believes that God created the world in six days, as described in Genesis

evolution by natural selection The theory that all life evolved (developed) from a common ancestor through gradual changes over millions of years

Genesis The first book of the Bible, which contains two accounts of how God created the world

myth A story that is not historically accurate, but contains spiritual truth

theistic evolution The belief that God started the process of evolution and uses it to bring about life

Check your understanding

1 Explain Darwin's theory.
2 Why is Darwin's theory unpopular with creationists?
3 Explain one way that a Christian might try to show that Genesis and evolution are both correct.
4 Explain why a Christian might think that the creation stories in Genesis are myths.
5 'It is not possible for both Darwin's theory and Genesis to be true.' Discuss.

Unit 1: Philosophy of religion

Why did Freud think God is all in the mind?

Why did the Austrian psychologist Sigmund Freud view religion as childish wishful thinking?

The Masters of Suspicion

In the 19th century, most Europeans were Christians who thought that religion was a good thing. However, there were three **atheists** who thought differently. In the books they wrote, their aim was to unmask and expose what they saw as the dark, unpleasant reality of belief in God. In the 1970s, they were given the name 'Masters of Suspicion' because of their suspicious and critical approach to religion.

Sigmund Freud

One 'Master of Suspicion' was the Austrian **psychologist Sigmund Freud**. Freud described religions as 'mass delusions' and tried to give a natural explanation for why people believe in God. He claimed that the reason is that religion satisfies three wishes or desires that all people have. Freud's theory is known as his **wish-fulfilment hypothesis.**

The Masters of Suspicion (left to right): Karl Marx (1818–1883), Friedrich Nietzsche (1844–1900) and Sigmund Freud (1856–1939)

The three wishes we all have (according to Freud)

1. The desire for a father

Freud believed that humans struggle to cope with the harsh, hostile and frightening reality of life. Our inability to cope with reality causes us to act in a childish way to make ourselves feel better. Instead of accepting reality, we imagine we have a loving and powerful father who will look after and protect us. This idea of a father can be seen in Christianity where Christians pray to a father who is viewed as loving and powerful.

2. The desire for fairness

According to Freud, all humans share a desire for fairness. We do not like the idea that bad people might get away with doing terrible things, or that good people do not get rewarded for the good things they do. Therefore, we convince ourselves that there is a God who sees everything and will either reward or punish each person when they die, depending on how they have lived.

3. The desire for immortality

The third universal human desire identified by Freud is the desire to be immortal (live forever). He thought that humans are too narcissistic (self-loving) to accept that we are simply animals that die and decay into the ground. Therefore, we tell ourselves that our actions on Earth matter to a higher being who will reward us with eternal life if we please him.

> ❝ The whole thing is so patently infantile, so foreign to reality, that to anyone with a friendly attitude to humanity, it is painful to think that the great majority of mortals will never be able to rise above this view of life. ❞
> Sigmund Freud, *Civilisation and Its Discontents* (1930)

A powerful but unhealthy solution

Freud thought that God was an illusion – that there is no God. He argued that the idea of God has power over us because it is passed down to us by our ancestors who were punished if they criticised it. The idea of God also helps us to cope with life by satisfying our strongest desires.

> ❝ Religions are illusions. Fulfilments of the oldest, strongest and most insistent wishes of mankind. The secret of their strength lies in the strength of those wishes. ❞
> Sigmund Freud, *The Future of an Illusion* (1927)

Sigmund Freud moved to London in 1938 and his house is now a museum. His study has been kept as it was during his life, including his famous couch on which patients would recline and tell him whatever thoughts came to mind.

Freud thought that religion was an unhealthy cure for the problem of fear because it causes people to go against their natural desires and instead focus on negative ideas such as sin and hell, which make them feel worse. He thought that for people to find true happiness, they must abandon religion.

Was Freud right?

Freud's wish-fulfilment hypothesis has been influential, but it has also been criticised because there is no evidence that all humans share the same desires. Furthermore, if Freud was right that humans do share these desires, it would not necessarily mean that God does not exist. It could be argued that, just as people desire water and oxygen because they are necessary and good for them, perhaps God deliberately made people to desire him so that they would seek him. It is possible, as Descartes thought, that the idea of God is imprinted on our minds by God.

Key vocabulary

atheist Someone who does not believe in the existence of a god or gods

psychologist Someone who studies human behaviour

wish-fulfilment hypothesis Freud's theory that religion is invented by humans to satisfy our desire for a father, for fairness and for immortality

Check your understanding

1. Who were the Masters of Suspicion and what did they have in common?
2. According to Freud's 'wish-fulfilment hypothesis', what three desires do all humans share and how does religion satisfy them?
3. Why did Freud believe that religion should be abandoned?
4. Why might Freud's wish-fulfilment hypothesis be criticised?
5. 'Freud's wish-fulfilment hypothesis is an unconvincing argument.' Discuss.

Unit 1: Philosophy of religion
Why did Marx compare religion to a drug?

Karl Marx compared religion to an addictive hallucinogenic drug. What point was he making and what led him to make this striking comparison?

The working class and ruling class

The German philosopher **Karl Marx** was an atheist who lived in the period following the Industrial Revolution, when people first began making goods in factories. Marx thought there were two classes of people in society: the **working class** and **ruling class**.

- The ruling class were wealthy, powerful people who owned land and factories.

- The working class were poor people who kept the ruling class rich by working for them.

Life was tough for the working class. In order to avoid starvation, men, women and children often worked 14-hour days in factories in difficult and dangerous conditions. If they quit, they might not find any other job. Their lives were short, often miserable, and they had little time to themselves. Meanwhile, the factory owners benefited from their hard work and grew rich.

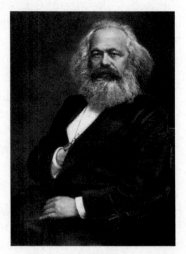

Karl Marx (1818–1883)

Marx claimed that the ruling class used religion as a way of controlling and manipulating the poor. They did this by telling the poor that it is more spiritual to be poor and that the poor will be rewarded in the afterlife. Evidence for this can be seen in the Bible where Paul warns that 'love of money is the root of all kinds of evil' and Jesus teaches that 'it is easier for a camel to go through the eye of a needle than for a rich person to enter the Kingdom of God!'

Marx disliked the idea that God favours and will reward those in poverty. He thought it distracted the working class from trying to improve their lives by causing them to focus on an imaginary afterlife where they will no longer suffer. Marx argued that religion creates a **false consciousness**: it distorts people's sense of reality so that they feel content with their lives. They believed that their poverty is what God wants rather than seeing the truth: that they were being **oppressed** by the rich and powerful ruling class.

The opium of the people

Marx described religion as the '**opium of the people**'. Opium is an addictive, painkilling drug that can cause hallucinations. By using the metaphor of opium, Marx was claiming that the working class become addicted to religious ideas as a way of numbing the pain of their earthly existence. Religion offers them the pleasant illusion of an afterlife and blinds them to their oppression. Marx described religion as a 'flight from inhuman working conditions' to make 'the misery of life more endurable'.

Revolution is the solution

Marx thought that rather than taking the painkilling drug of religion, the working class needed to become aware of the fact that they were being oppressed. He called this awareness **class consciousness**. When the working class achieved class consciousness, Marx argued, they would overthrow the ruling class in a **revolution** and create a classless society in which everybody was equal. In this society, there would be no need for religion as its sole purpose is to help the ruling class keep power and to make life less miserable for the working class. Only in such a society could real happiness be found. Marx's ideas inspired revolutions in Russia and China, and many people around the world today, influenced by his ideas, call themselves Marxists.

> ❝ Religion is the sigh of the oppressed creature, the heart of a heartless world, and the soul of soulless conditions. It is the opium of the people. The abolition of religion as the illusory happiness of the people is the demand for their real happiness. ❞
>
> Karl Marx, *A Contribution to the Critique of Hegel's Philosophy of Right* (1844)

The Soviet Union

Vladimir Lenin became the first leader of the Soviet Union (USSR) in 1922. He was strongly influenced by the ideas of Marx. He described religion as 'spiritual gin' that created a 'mystical fog'. Like Marx, he believed that religion was a way of controlling and confusing the majority of people in order for the minority to keep their power and wealth. When Lenin became leader, most people in the Soviet Union were Christian. He aimed to rid the Soviet Union of religion and replace it with atheism. Religion was ridiculed, religious property was confiscated and children were taught in school that they should be atheists. Between 1922 and 1926, 28 bishops and over 1200 priests were killed. When the Soviet Union broke up into 15 separate countries in 1991, the vast majority of the population were atheists.

Vladimir Lenin (1870–1924)

Key vocabulary

class consciousness A term used by Marx to mean the working class becoming aware they are being oppressed

false consciousness A term used by Marx to describe a way of thinking that stops the working class from seeing how they are being oppressed

opium of the people A phrase used by Marx comparing religion to opium, an addictive, painkilling and vision-creating drug

oppress Use power to keep someone in a bad situation

revolution Overthrowing those in power in order to cause change

ruling class According to Marx, the minority of rich and powerful people, such as factory owners

working class According to Marx, the mass of poor people who work for (and are oppressed by) the ruling class

Check your understanding

1 Who were the two classes in society according to Marx and what was life like for them?

2 Why did Marx dislike religion?

3 Why did Marx use the metaphor of opium to describe religion?

4 What did Marx think needed to happen in order for society to improve? (Use the terms 'false consciousness' and 'class consciousness' in your answer.)

5 What did Lenin believe about religion and how did he put his belief into action in the Soviet Union?

Unit 1: Philosophy of religion
Does the idea of God make sense?

Is it possible for God to be completely powerful, knowledgeable and loving?

The paradox of omnipotence

Some people say that it is impossible for an **omnipotent** god to exist because omnipotence is illogical. This is often illustrated by the following example:

> **Q:** Can God create a rock that is too heavy for him to lift?

> **A:** Yes. This means he is not omnipotent because there is something he cannot lift.

> **A:** No. This means he is not omnipotent because there is something he cannot create.

Some people argue that God cannot create a rock too heavy for him to lift, but this is not because God is not omnipotent; it is because the idea of a rock that God cannot lift is illogical, in the same way that God cannot create a square triangle, achieve 11/10 in a test or create a dog that is also a fish. Others argue that God is not limited by logic in the way that humans are. If there are things that God cannot do, then he cannot be omnipotent because there is something more powerful than him. Others argue that omnipotent means being the most powerful being in the universe, but not being able to do anything.

The question of whether it is possible for God to be all-powerful is known as the 'paradox of omnipotence'.

Can God be omniscient if humans are free?

Some people also argue that God cannot be **omniscient** if humans have **free will**. This is because if God knows with absolute certainty what we are going to do in the future, then there is nothing that we can do to change what is going to happen. For example, if God knows for certain that you are going to tell a lie tomorrow, then it is already fixed that you will do this and you cannot not do it. If we do not have free will, it seems unfair for God to judge us for our actions because we are not able to choose to do otherwise. Others argue that it is possible for God to know what we will freely choose to do without in any way controlling it.

If God knows everything, is it possible for humans to be free?

Why doesn't God stop suffering?

Many people argue that if God was truly **omnibenevolent** and omnipotent, then there would be no suffering in the world. The suffering caused both by natural disasters and disease as well as human actions show that there is no God – or at least not an omnibenevolent, omnipotent and omniscient one. This is known as the **problem of evil**.

In response, religious philosophers argue that it is possible for there to be a good reason why an omnibenevolent god would allow evil and suffering. It could be to test and strengthen people's belief in God, to help their character grow or because to stop suffering would require God to take away our free will, which would be unloving. Perhaps a world where humans are free, but can choose to do evil is the best possible world. This is because a world where people's actions had neither good nor bad intentions would be a world where neither good nor evil would be possible. It would simply be a bland, neutral world where no action had any meaning.

For some people, the problem of evil is enough to convince them that God does not exist. Others argue that the only way we could know why an omnipotent, omnibenevolent god would allow evil is if we knew what omnipotent, omnibenevolent gods usually do, or if we were this god. As neither of these is possible, the reason why God allows evil and suffering remains a mystery, but our inability to know the reason does not mean that there is not a good one.

However, some people would say that defending God by saying he is a mystery is an unsatisfactory way of resolving the problem of evil. In response, it could be argued that the view we should be able to understand an infinite god with finite minds, is equally unreasonable. This point was made by a 5th-century Christian philosopher named Augustine, who claimed that if you think you have fully understood God, you are wrong; you have simply understood your own invented idea of God.

> 66 If you think you have grasped him, it is not God you have grasped. 99
> St Augustine of Hippo

Key vocabulary

apophatic theology The view that God cannot be accurately described in positive language, only by saying what God is not

free will The ability to choose between right and wrong

omnibenevolent All-loving

omnipotent All-powerful

omniscient All-knowing

problem of evil The argument that evil and suffering shows that an omnipotent, omniscient, omnibenevolent god does not exist

Watch your language

Some philosophers argue that the problems described above arise because our language is too limited to express the essence of God. There is nothing that we can say that accurately expresses what God is like. Therefore, some Christians think that they should only talk about what God is _not_, rather than what he is. This is known as **apophatic theology**. For example, they would say that God is not bad and not weak, but neither is he good or powerful, because this limits God to ideas of good and powerful that we use to describe imperfect things in the world.

Some would go as far as saying 'God is nothing'. They do not mean that God is not real, but that there is literally no 'thing' in the universe that can be used to describe God because he is completely different from everything that exists. He is in a category of his own and is not describable or even fully knowable by human senses or reason.

Check your understanding

1. Explain two ways that a religious person might understand omnipotence.
2. Do you think it is possible for humans to have free will if there is an omniscient god?
3. Explain two ways that a religious person might defend God against the problem of evil.
4. Explain why some people believe in apophatic theology.
5. 'The idea of God does not make sense.' Discuss.

Are the New Atheists right about faith?

Is faith needed to understand reality? Or is faith simply an excuse for believing in God when reasons fail?

What is New Atheism?

In 2004, the atheist scientist Richard Dawkins wrote a book called *The God Delusion* claiming that people who believe in God are deluded. In the years that followed, three other atheists wrote similar books criticising belief in God. These four – Richard Dawkins (UK), Sam Harris (USA), Christopher Hitchens (UK, died in 2011) and Daniel Dennett (USA) – were named the **New Atheists** by the media. Unlike many atheists before them who have ignored religion as something of no interest to them, the New Atheists are very critical of religion. They think that religious beliefs and ideas should not be shown a special respect or tolerance. People should feel free to challenge and criticise religious ideas in the same way that they feel free to criticise others' ideas about which is the best football team, musician or political party.

Richard Dawkins (born 1941)

Can science answer the question of God's existence?

The New Atheists believe that everything can be explained naturally. They view the question of whether God exists as a scientific question that people should answer based on scientific evidence. However, many atheists and religious people disagree; they argue that science is limited to explaining natural, material things, not spiritual things that are outside the universe like God. Trying to answer the question of God's existence with science is like trying to prove or disprove the existence of oxygen with a metal detector. God is not the same as other existing things, such as gravity, a table or an animal. Therefore, God's existence cannot be tested for in the same way.

Christopher Hitchens (1949-2011)

> 66 We cannot, of course, disprove God, just as we can't disprove Thor, fairies, leprechauns and the Flying Spaghetti Monster. But, like those other fantasies which we can't disprove, we can say that God is very, very improbable. 99
>
> Richard Dawkins

> 66 Exceptional claims demand exceptional evidence… what can be asserted without evidence can also be dismissed without evidence. 99
>
> Christopher Hitchens

Daniel Dennett (born 1942)

Richard Dawkins claims: '**Faith** is the great cop out, the great excuse to evade the need to think and evaluate evidence. Faith is belief in spite of, even perhaps because of, the lack of evidence.' Similarly, Sam Harris claims that faith is simply an excuse that religious people give each other 'to keep believing when reasons fail'. However, many would argue that the New Atheists misrepresent religious faith. Believers in God might say that there are arguments that make faith reasonable, and faith is just a final leap, required when evidence is inconclusive. These believers might argue that it is more probable that God exists, and so it is reasonable for them to have faith in God.

Religious people might argue that life is full of uncertain choices about what we should think and do, and we make choices based on reasonable trust or faith rather than proof. For example, when we sit on a chair, we have reasonable trust it will support us; we do not try to prove it first. We think that the sun will continue to rise and seasons will continue in the same order, but this requires faith that the future will be the same as the past. We have faith that we exist and that we are not dreaming, and people have faith that their parents or partner love them even though they cannot be certain. Perhaps, therefore, faith is a necessary way of understanding the world in order to prevent ourselves living in constant doubt and uncertainty.

Some religious people argue that God deliberately remains distant from us so that we can be free to choose to have faith. If we had complete and convincing evidence that God exists, then faith would have little value and we would perhaps lose the ability to reject the existence of God.

The question of whether there is a god, gods or some other sort of higher power has preoccupied human minds for millennia. For many religious people, they would say that it is by having faith in God and by following him that they become more and more certain of his existence. However, with so many different views on what counts as reliable knowledge or acceptable proof, the question of God's existence remains fiercely debated.

Key vocabulary

faith Belief or trust in something that cannot be proven

Pascal's wager

The 17th-century French mathematician and philosopher **Blaise Pascal** thought that nobody can know for certain whether God exists. It is a gamble whatever decision you make; therefore, you should think about what you risk winning and losing. If you gamble that God exists, you stand to win a place in paradise forever; if you are wrong, you lose nothing. If you gamble that God does _not_ exist and are right, you win nothing because there is no afterlife; however, if you are wrong, then you do not get a place in heaven. As such, Pascal thought that the more sensible decision was to believe that God exists. His theory is known as Pascal's wager.

Blaise Pascal (1623–1662)

Check your understanding

1 Who are the New Atheists and what do they have in common?

2 Why might a religious person argue that God's existence is not a scientific question?

3 Explain why the New Atheists criticise faith and how religious people might respond.

4 Explain Pascal's wager. Do you agree with him?

5 'There are no good reasons to believe in God.' Discuss.

What do people in the UK believe?

How religious are people in the UK today?

What is a 'none'?

Approximately 84 per cent of people in the world today follow a religion, and experts predict that this will rise to 87 per cent by 2050. However, in the UK, people are becoming less religious.

It is difficult to know precisely what all the people in a country believe, but one way of finding out is through surveys. In the government census, people are asked the question: 'What is your religion?' They can choose to state which religion they follow or to select 'no religion'. In the 2011 census, 25 per cent of people ticked 'no religion' – this was 10 per cent higher than the previous census in 2001. There are also smaller surveys, such as the British Social Attitudes Survey, in which 52 per cent of people stated that they follow no religion in 2017.

The name given to the category of people who follow no religion is **nones**. However, despite being part of the same category, nones do not all believe the same things or live in the same way.

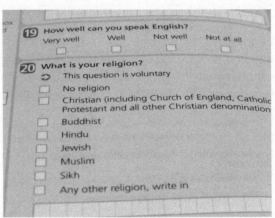

In the 2011 UK census, approximately 10 per cent of people described themselves as followers of a religion other than Christianity. Islam was the second most popular religion with 5 per cent of people describing themselves as Muslims. Between 2001 and 2011, the number of people ticking Christianity fell from 72 per cent to 59 per cent.

Atheism and agnosticism

Some nones are atheists, meaning that they do not believe in the existence of a god or gods. Others would describe themselves as **agnostic**, which means they do not know whether there is a god or gods. An agnostic might be personally unsure about whether there is a god, or they might believe it is impossible for anybody to know.

Unlike followers of religions, atheists and agnostics do not have a shared text, a common set of beliefs or agreed instructions about how to live. They decide what to believe and how to live for themselves. Different atheists and different agnostics can therefore have little in common. Some believe that religion is a bad thing, as the New Atheists do. Others are not opposed to religion; they just do not believe in the existence of a higher power or simply do not have any interest in religion.

Spiritual but not religious (SBNR)

Some nones would describe themselves as spiritual but not religious (SBNR). They might believe in a higher power but choose not to follow a religion. This could be because they disagree with the teachings and texts of religions, or because they are put off by discrimination or violence done in the name of religion.

Somebody who is SBNR might be a 'spiritual shopper' creating a 'pick 'n' mix' worldview. This means that they pick beliefs and ways of living from different religions to create their own individual way of viewing the world. For example, a none who is SBNR might have a non-religious wedding but believe in an afterlife and pray to a higher power in a similar way to Christians. In addition, they might practise meditation and yoga, which are more commonly found in Hinduism and Buddhism.

What is humanism?

Some atheists describe themselves as **humanists**. Humanists believe that there is no afterlife and so we should make the most of the one life that we have on Earth. They believe that we should use science and our reason, rather than religion, to understand the world. They also believe that we should show compassion to other people and so oppose discrimination and encourage equality.

Humanists UK

Humanists UK is a humanist organisation that campaigns for the UK to become a secular (non-religious) country. They believe that religion should not be given special treatment in society and that faith schools should be abolished. In the past, they have campaigned for people who do not follow a religion to tick 'no religion' in the UK census; this, they argue, is to prevent inaccurate statistics being used to defend special treatment being given to religion in society.

Humanists UK also provide training to members of their organisation who want to be able to conduct humanist weddings, funerals and baby-naming ceremonies, which focus on humanist ideas about life rather than religious ideas.

In 2009, £150 000 was donated to Humanists UK to fund advertising on buses around the UK and on the London underground in response to Christian advertising on buses.

Key vocabulary

agnostic Someone who does not know whether there is a god or gods

humanist An atheist who believes that science and our shared human reason and compassion should guide how we live the one life that we have

nones A term used by sociologists (people who study society) to describe the diverse group of people with no religion, including atheists, agnostics and those who are spiritual but not religious

Check your understanding

1 How do we know what people believe in the UK?

2 What is the difference between an agnostic and an atheist?

3 Explain what somebody who is spiritual but not religious might believe.

4 Explain what humanists believe and how this might impact the way they live.

5 'The atheist bus campaign was unnecessary.' Discuss.

Unit 1: Philosophy of religion
Knowledge organiser

Key vocabulary

agnostic Someone who does not know whether there is a god or gods

apophatic theology The view that God cannot be accurately described in positive language, only by saying what God is not

atheist Someone who does not believe in the existence of a god or gods

class consciousness A term used by Marx to mean the working class becoming aware they are being oppressed

creationist Someone who believes that God created the world in six days, as described in Genesis

Design (or teleological) argument The argument that the world looks designed and so has a designer – God

empiricism The theory that knowledge is gained through our five senses

evolution by natural selection The theory that all life evolved (developed) from a common ancestor through gradual changes over millions of years

faith Belief or trust in something that cannot be proven

fallacy of composition An argument that wrongly claims that what is true of something's parts must also be true of the whole thing

false consciousness A term used by Marx to describe a way of thinking that stops the working class from seeing how they are being oppressed

First Cause argument The argument that everything in the universe needs a cause and so the universe also needs a cause, which is God

first certainty 'I think; therefore I am': Descartes' realisation that the fact he thinks shows that his mind must exist

free will The ability to choose between right and wrong

Genesis The first book of the Bible, which contains two accounts of how God created the world

Gospels The first four books of the New Testament in the Bible which describe the life and teachings of Jesus

humanist An atheist who believes that science and our shared human reason and compassion should guide how we live the one life that we have

infinite regress An endless sequence of causes with no beginning

logical fallacy A statement that is logically flawed

miracle An event that cannot be explained naturally and so is seen as an act of a god or gods

myth A story that is not historically accurate, but contains spiritual truth

nones A term used by sociologists (people who study society) to describe the diverse group of people with no religion, including atheists, agnostics and those who are spiritual but not religious

omnibenevolent All-loving

omnipotent All-powerful

omniscient All-knowing

opium of the people A phrase used by Marx comparing religion to opium, an addictive, painkilling and vision-creating drug

oppress Use power to keep someone in a bad situation

problem of evil The argument that evil and suffering shows that an omnipotent, omniscient, omnibenevolent god does not exist

psychologist Someone who studies human behaviour

rationalism The theory that knowledge is gained through reason

Realm of Appearances Plato's name for the world in which we live

Realm of Forms Plato's name for a perfect realm where our souls previously lived

revolution Overthrowing those in power in order to cause change

ruling class According to Marx, the minority of rich and powerful people, such as factory owners

theistic evolution The belief that God started the process of evolution and uses it to bring about life

trademark argument Descartes' argument that humans are born with the idea of God imprinted on their minds

wish-fulfilment hypothesis Freud's theory that religion is invented by humans in order to satisfy our desire for a father, for fairness and for immortality

working class According to Marx, the mass of poor people who work for (and are oppressed by) the ruling class

Charles Darwin.

Key people

Aristotle Ancient Greek philosopher (4th century BCE) and student of Plato who thought that knowledge is gained through our senses (empiricism)

Thomas Aquinas 13th-century Italian philosopher and priest whose *Summa Theologica* outlines his 'Five Ways' of demonstrating that faith in God is reasonable, including the First Cause argument

Charles Darwin 19th-century scientist and author of *On the Origin of Species* in 1859, which outlined his theory of evolution by natural selection

René Descartes 16th-century French philosopher who claimed that his ability to think proved he must exist

Sigmund Freud 19th/20th-century Austrian psychologist who claimed in his wish-fulfilment hypothesis that humans invent religion to satisfy their desires for a father, fairness and immortality

David Hume 18th-century Scottish philosopher who criticised the first cause and design arguments and belief in miracles

Karl Marx 19th-century German philosopher who described religion as the 'opium of the people', used by the ruling class to exploit and oppress the working class

New Atheists Four modern thinkers and writers from the UK and USA (including Richard Dawkins, author of *The God Delusion*) who criticise faith and argue that science and reason can answer all questions about the universe

William Paley 18th-century English philosopher and priest who compared the world to a watch in his version of the design argument

Blaise Pascal 17th-century French philosopher who argued that, when deciding whether or not God exists, it is more sensible to gamble that he does because of the potential reward in the afterlife (known as Pascal's wager)

Plato Ancient Greek philosopher (4th-century BCE) who claimed that knowledge is gained through using reason (rationalism)

Unit 1: Philosophy of religion
End of unit quiz

1. Which Ancient Greek philosopher believed in the Realm of Appearances and the Realm of Forms?

2. What is the name given to the theory that knowledge is gained through our five senses?

3. What is the name given to the theory that knowledge is gained through reason?

4. Which French philosopher claimed in his first certainty that having the thought that he might not exist proved that his mind existed?

5. What is the name of the argument that humans are born with the idea of God imprinted or tattooed on their minds?

6. Which Italian philosopher outlined his 'First Cause argument' in *Summa Theologica*?

7. Which Scottish philosopher claimed that the First Cause argument was based on the fallacy of composition?

8. What is the name of the argument made by William Paley that the appearance of design in the world shows there must be an intelligent designer?

9. What word means an event that is not explainable naturally and so is seen as an act of a god or gods?

10. What was the name of Charles Darwin's book in which he explained his theory of evolution by natural selection?

11. What name is given to someone who interprets the Genesis creation story literally?

12. What is a myth?

13. What name is given to someone who does not believe in a god or gods?

14. Which Austrian psychologist described religion as 'infantile wish fulfilment'?

15. What three wishes or desires did this psychologist think that all humans share?

16. What phrase did the German philosopher Karl Marx use to describe religion?

17. Give one reason why he said this.

18. What did Marx think the working class would do to solve their problem once they achieved class consciousness?

19. What word means 'all-powerful'?

20. What word means 'all-knowing'?

21. What word means 'all-loving'?

22. What term means 'the ability to choose between right and wrong'?

23. What is the 'problem of evil'?

24. What is the name given to the view that we cannot describe God in positive language; we can only say what God is _not_?

25. What word means belief or trust in something that cannot be conclusively proven?

26. What is the name given by the media to the four modern thinkers and writers who criticise belief in God because it lacks evidence?

27. Which French philosopher said that we cannot be certain whether God exists, so we should wager or gamble that he does because there is more to win and less to lose?

28. What is the name given by sociologists to the diverse group of people who do not follow a religion?

29. What name is given to someone who does not know whether a god exists?

30. State two beliefs of humanists.

Ethics

How should we live our lives? Is there a best way to live? Are some actions always right or wrong, or does it depend on the situation or consequences? What about our human nature? Is it good or bad, or neither? What even are we as humans? Are we simply physical matter and does that affect how we think about right and wrong? If we are just physical matter, could and should we create artificial intelligence like us? If we do, should this artificial intelligence have rights and responsibilities? And what about animals? Are we more important than them, or is to argue that simply speciesism?

These are just a few of the questions that you will be examining over the course of this unit. In doing so, you will gain knowledge of some of the key ideas and arguments that have informed ethical debate through history and continue to influence the way people think and act in the modern world.

Driving

Unit 2: Ethics
What is ethics?

How do we know what is right and wrong?

How should we live?

Throughout history, people have wondered how to live a 'good' life. Christians and Muslims believe that God has revealed how to live a good life to humans, and he will judge them after death on how they have lived. Similarly, Hindus and Buddhists believe that good actions in this life will result in a good rebirth when they die. However, for people who believe there is no god and we only have one life, other ways are needed to decide how to live the best or right way.

The name given to people's principles or views on right and wrong is **morality**. A person's morality might be influenced by their religion, family, friends and the society in which they live. The area of philosophy that explores the nature of morality and how moral decisions should be made is called **ethics**.

Where does morality come from?

Some people believe that morality is innate, meaning inbuilt. In other words, we are born with a natural sense of right and wrong. If morality is innate, this would, in theory, mean that if someone were to grow up in isolation away from all other humans, they would still have a sense of right and wrong. However, humans' moral views have varied greatly in different places and different points in history. For example, 2500 years ago in Ancient Greece, Spartans would bathe their babies in wine rather than water to see how they reacted. If the baby seemed weak, they would not be useful in battle and so would be left on a hillside to die. Nowadays, there are some parts of the world where people believe that the death penalty is right and other parts, such as the UK, where it has been abolished. These big differences in opinion could suggest that morality is not innate.

The morality of the Spartans was different from modern Western morality.

John Locke's 'blank slate'

The 17th-century English philosopher, **John Locke**, argued that we are born with no knowledge of anything; a new-born baby's mind is like a blank slate (*tabula rasa*). All of our knowledge comes from experiences that are written on to the 'blank slate' of our mind.

Some modern scientists would disagree with Locke's view that we are born with no knowledge; they would say that we are born with a desire to survive and pass on our genes. This motivates us to act in ways that benefit us. Therefore, perhaps we have developed morality so that we work together to make society a safe, pleasant place where we will survive and flourish.

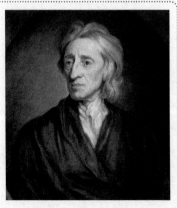
John Locke (1632–1704)

Does altruism exist?

Some philosophers who believe humans are simply driven by a selfish desire to survive argue that **altruism** (selflessness) does not exist. All of our actions that appear altruistic, such as giving to charity or risking our lives for others, are simply selfishness in disguise. This is the view of American scientist Michael Ghiselin (born 1939) who famously said, 'scratch an altruist and watch a hypocrite bleed'. Ghiselin meant that if you scratch below the surface and look a bit deeper, someone who appears to be acting in a selfless way will always have selfish motives.

Some people might argue that whether a person's motives are selfish or not makes no difference to whether an action is good or bad. Others would say that motive does matter, and so a good action done with a bad intention is in some way less good than the same action done with a good intention.

What makes an action good or bad?

Some people believe that actions are inherently good or bad. This means that actions are good or bad in themselves regardless of their consequence. This view is known as **absolutism**. For example, murder or lying might always be seen as bad, while kindness and honesty might always be seen as good.

Others would argue that no action is always good or bad; it depends on the situation and the action's consequences. This is known as **relativism**. An absolutist would argue that something like lying is always wrong, whereas a relativist would argue that there are situations where lying might be right – for example, if it protected someone from being hurt.

Do right and wrong really exist?

Some people would argue that good and evil do not really exist; they are just words people use to express behaviour they like and do not like. Rather than being something fixed for all people at all times, morality is simply what a person or culture prefers; it is just fashion. For example, if I say 'lying is wrong', all I am really saying is 'I don't like lying'. For those who hold this view, there is no way of saying that one morality is any better than any other. There is simply difference, without any way of judging between them.

> **Think**
>
> Are there some things that are always right or wrong? Why is this? How do you know your answer is correct?

> **Key vocabulary**
>
> **absolutism** The view that certain actions are inherently good or bad
>
> **altruism** Selfless actions done without thought or expectation of a reward
>
> **ethics** The philosophical study of right and wrong
>
> **morality** Ideas or principles about what is right and wrong
>
> **relativism** The view that whether an action is good or bad depends on the situation

---

Check your understanding

1 What is meant by morality and what sort of things might influence it?

2 With examples, explain why the view that morality is innate might be criticised.

3 Why might a scientist disagree with John Locke's view of humans?

4 Explain the difference between absolutism and relativism.

5 'Altruism does not exist, but it does not matter.' Discuss.

How should we live if God is dead?

Why did Friedrich Nietzsche accuse atheists of acting like Christians?

'God is dead'

Friedrich Nietzsche was a German atheist, famous for stating that 'God is dead, and we have killed him'. Nietzsche was not trying to say that humans had literally killed God. He meant that the idea of God was no longer necessary or plausible (believable) because science could now answer difficult questions about human existence instead.

Friedrich Nietzsche (1844–1900)

> 66 We have killed him – you and I. We are all his murderers. But how have we done this? How were we able to drink up the sea? Who gave us the sponge to wipe away the entire horizon?...God is dead. God remains dead. And we have killed him. 99
>
> Friedrich Nietzsche

The death of morality

Nietzsche thought that the death of God should have dramatic consequences for how humans live. Christians believe that God decides what is right and wrong and reveals it to humans, but if God does not really exist, then it makes no sense to follow his rules or ideas. For example, there is no longer any need or reason to believe in forgiveness, caring for the weak or human equality. The death of God frees people to rethink how to live. It allows us to start afresh and create a new, more natural morality that reflects our true human nature.

Fact

The line for which Nietzsche is best known, 'God is dead, and we have killed him', was actually taken from a popular Christian hymn about Jesus' crucifixion.

The Ten Commandments, found in Jewish and Christian scripture, set out ten 'rules' for leading a moral life.

Christian morality is influenced by Genesis 1, which states that humans are made in the 'image of God' and so every human life has equal worth. In Jesus' parables and sermons, he taught that people should care for the weak and needy, forgive endlessly and avoid revenge: for example, 'love your enemies, pray for those who persecute you' and 'if someone slaps you on one cheek, turn the other cheek'.

The will to power and the enemy of life

Nietzsche believed that humans are driven by a desire for strength and power. He called this **the will to power**. Nietzsche thought that Christian morality was invented by weak, powerless people in order to control strong, powerful people. The weak trick strong people into believing that qualities such as selflessness, humility, forgiveness, equality and caring for the weak are 'good' whereas the actions that the strong, powerful people would naturally do are 'sinful' or 'evil'. This means that instead of living naturally, the strong are tricked into acting against their human nature and behaving in weak, unnatural ways to be 'good' and avoid sin. This is why Nietzsche described Christian morality as 'the enemy of life' and a 'crime against life'. Nietzsche hated the idea of sin because he thought it causes humans to feel ashamed of their natural instincts and dislike themselves.

The doctrine of eternal recurrence

Nietzsche thought that if people wanted to know whether they were living a good life, they should ask themselves whether they would be willing for their life to repeat itself in exactly the same way over and over. If they would have regrets or be unhappy with their choices, then they were not living a good life. He called this idea 'the doctrine of eternal recurrence'. Nietzsche thought that only the truly strong people could accept the doctrine of eternal recurrence because it requires people to love life and accept the physical world as it is rather than find comfort in an imaginary god or illusory afterlife. He imagined a future stage of human development where there would be a higher form of being called an Übermensch (Superman) whose hatred of weakness would lead him to defeat it and create his own strong morals.

Was Nietzsche right?

Many atheists would argue that the morals that Nietzsche viewed as 'Christian' were not really Christian morals, but simply good and natural human morals. Therefore, atheists do not need to abandon their morality simply because they do not believe in the Christian God. Some philosophers have argued that humans are not motivated by power, but actually want to care for others and create equality. Their ideas influence humanists, who believe that people should use their natural reason, empathy and respect for others to make the world a better place for everyone. A humanist might argue that Nietzsche's ideas would lead to inequality and suffering, making the world a far less pleasant place for most people to live.

> Nietzsche wrote: 'It is no surprise that lambs do not like great birds of prey.' However, he didn't think that we should see great birds of prey as evil because they attack lambs. In the same way, people who are naturally strong and powerful should not be seen as evil for demonstrating their strength over others.

Key vocabulary

the will to power A term used by Nietzsche to describe a natural human desire for strength and power

---

Check your understanding

1 Who was Friedrich Nietzsche and what did he mean by 'God is dead, and we have killed him'?

2 Explain why Nietzsche thought that the 'death of God' was a good thing.

3 Explain Nietzsche's doctrine of eternal recurrence.

4 Why might a humanist disagree with Nietzsche?

5 'Nietzsche's ideas are wrong and the world would be a worse place if everyone followed them.' Discuss.

Unit 2: Ethics
Are goodness and pleasure the same?

Should we decide if actions are right or wrong based on whether they produce pleasure?

What is utilitarianism?

The 18th-century English philosopher **Jeremy Bentham** was an atheist, who did not think that God decides which actions are good or bad. Nor did Bentham think that goodness was about protecting people's rights. He described the idea that people naturally possess rights as 'nonsense on stilts'. Bentham thought that humans are simple creatures, motivated by the desire to avoid pain and experience pleasure. Therefore, when deciding on whether an action is good or bad, we should simply focus on how much pleasure or pain it will cause. If an action causes more pleasure than suffering, it should be viewed as good; if an action causes more suffering than pleasure, then it should be viewed as bad. Bentham's theory is known as **utilitarianism**.

Jeremy Bentham (1748–1832)

Utilitarians think that the best action in any situation is the one that creates the greatest amount of pleasure or good for the greatest number of people. They are relativists, meaning they believe that no action is good or bad in all circumstances; whether an action is good or bad depends on its context and consequences.

> 66 Nature has placed mankind under the governance of two sovereign masters, pain and pleasure. It is for them alone to point out what we shall do. 99
> Jeremy Bentham, *An Introduction to the Principles of Morals and Legislation* (1789)

The hedonic calculus

A difficulty with utiltarianism is that it is hard to measure happiness. To solve this, Bentham created a method of calculating happiness called the **hedonic calculus**. This involves considering on one side all the pleasure an action might produce and on the other side, any pain that it might cause. The amount of pain should then be subtracted from the amount of pleasure to find what Bentham called the 'utility' (usefulness) of an action – the more pleasure an action creates, the more useful it is. If there is no other action that creates a higher happiness value, then you have found the best action.

Bentham: A radical thinker

Bentham's theory was radical because it was based on the idea that everyone's happiness was equally important; nobody's happiness was valued more highly because of their wealth or place in society. Although controversial at the time, Bentham's theory influences the way that governments make decisions today.

Was Bentham right?

Bentham suggested that calculating happiness is as easy as calculating a mathematical sum. However, units of pleasure and pain are hard to quantify and often depend on an individual's opinion. Also, we cannot predict the future and so can never be certain of what the consequences of an action will be. Furthermore, there is often not time to apply the hedonic calculus to decisions, which reduces its usefulness. Some utilitarians would respond to this by saying that general rules should be created that work most of the time, rather than individuals working out what is right and wrong in every situation.

Critics of utilitarianism argue that right and wrong cannot simply be reduced to pleasure and pain; morality is more complicated than this and other things need to be considered. Bentham's view that no actions are always wrong and human rights do not exist could be used to justify cruelty to an individual or minority group if it created happiness for the majority. For example, if three prison guards took pleasure in torturing a prisoner, this would be allowed because it causes happiness to a greater number. Equally, if imprisoning an innocent person would make the inhabitants of a village feel safer after a crime had been committed, then there would be no reason not to do this.

A 19th-century philosopher, **John Stuart Mill**, developed his own version of Bentham's theory that partly aimed to address this problem. Mill argued that there are both 'higher pleasures' and 'lower pleasures'. For example, he thought the pleasure to be found in reading Shakespeare is higher than the pleasure of a pig rolling in mud. He thought that it is not the _quantity_ or amount of pleasure produced by an action, but the _quality_ of the pleasure produced that is most important. However, deciding which pleasures should be viewed as higher and lower causes much disagreement.

To help keep his ideas alive, Bentham wanted his body to be stuffed and put on display after his death. His preserved body can be found sitting on a chair in a glass box at University College London. His real head has been replaced with a wax one.

Robert Nozick's experience machine

An American philosopher, **Robert Nozick** (1938–2002) disagreed with utilitarianism. He claimed that, if it were possible to attach electrodes permanently to our brain that could trick us into thinking and feeling we were having any pleasurable experience we wanted, such as making a new friend or reading a book, many people would not choose to do it. This is because we want to actually _do_ certain things and _be_ certain sorts of people, for example, brave, intelligent and funny, not simply experience these as a result of deluded thoughts. Furthermore, plugging into the machine would limit us to experiencing an artificial reality that we had created for ourselves rather than true reality. Nozick thought that this shows that goodness cannot be reduced simply to pleasure; humans desire and value more than this.

Key vocabulary

hedonic calculus Jeremy Bentham's way of calculating which actions are right and wrong

utilitarianism The theory that the best action in any situation is the one which creates the greatest amount of good for the greatest number

Check your understanding

1 What is utilitarianism?

2 Explain how the hedonic calculus works.

3 Why were Bentham's ideas radical and what happened after his death to keep them alive?

4 Explain two criticisms of utilitarianism.

5 'Utilitarianism is a helpful way of deciding what is right and wrong'. Discuss.

Unit 2: Ethics
What should we do with the runaway train?

Why did Philippa Foot think morality should not be based on the consequences of an action?

Philippa Foot's runaway train thought experiment

Imagine you are standing on a railway bridge. Beneath you are five workers repairing the railway track. Either side of the track are slopes that are too steep and high to climb. Coming around the corner is a runaway train without a driver. It is hurtling towards the workers and they are certain to die. Next to you is a lever. If you pull the lever, it will cause the train to divert onto a separate track and the five people will be saved. However, there is one worker on the separate track who will be killed if you divert the train. You have two options and seconds to decide. Should you pull the lever?

Philippa Foot devised the original version of the train problem.

This is what is known as a **thought experiment** and was first created in 1967 by an English philosopher called **Philippa Foot**.

An absolutist might think that to actively do something that will kill one person is worse than not interfering and letting five people die. Therefore, they would say the right thing to do is to stand back and do nothing. However, most people would pull the lever and divert the train because they think it is better for one person to be killed than five.

Should you kill the heavy man?

Imagine you are on the railway bridge again. This time, there is a heavy man standing next to you. If you push him onto the tracks, it will cause the train to stop before it reaches the five people. However, it will cause the heavy man to die. Should you throw the heavy man off the bridge? If not, how is killing the heavy man to save five people any different to pulling a lever to redirect the train and save five people?

Is our morality consistent?

Philippa Foot created the runaway train thought experiment because she wanted to explore why people think it is right to kill a person to save others in some situations, but not in others. In her view, the thought experiment showed that the consequences of an action cannot be all that determines whether an action is right or wrong. Therefore, ethical theories such as utilitarianism are flawed.

> ## Think
>
> Would you pull the lever? Would you change your mind if one of the workers was a friend or relative? How would you justify your decision?

Philippa Foot (1920–2010)

Foot gave another example to demonstrate this point. Imagine you are a surgeon. You have five patients who are all going to die if they do not receive a transplant that day. Two of the patients need one lung each, two need a kidney each and the other patient needs a heart. A healthy young man walks into the hospital with all five things that are needed. If you chop him open and take out his organs, the other five people will be saved, but the young man will die. You ask the man if he is willing for this to happen, but he says he is not. Should you kill the healthy young man anyway to save the five people? Most people would think it wrong for the doctor to ignore the young man's request and kill him to take his organs. However, Foot wondered why we view this differently to killing one person on the train tracks in order to save five others.

Foot gave a further example. Imagine you are a judge. An unknown person has committed a crime. Rioters have taken five innocent people hostage. They are going to kill the five hostages unless you hold a trial and someone is executed for the crime. You only have two options. Should you let the rioters kill the five hostages, or should you accuse an innocent person of the crime and sentence them to death in order to save the five hostages? Again, most people think that it would be wrong for the judge to sentence an innocent person to death, but this seems inconsistent with a willingness to pull a lever to kill one worker on the train tracks.

The ethics of programming driverless cars

The ethical questions raised by the runaway train are similar to those facing people who programme decisions into driverless cars. For example, if a driverless car's brakes fail forcing it to crash into an equal number of people whichever way it turns, how should it choose which way to crash? Should humans be prioritised over animals? Children over adults? Pedestrians over passengers? Furthermore, who is responsible for any of those deaths? Perhaps most importantly, who should have the power to choose the decisions that are programmed into the car?

The invention of driverless cars raises many ethical questions.

Key vocabulary

thought experiment
An imaginary scenario invented to examine the consequences of a philosophical idea

Check your understanding

1 In each of the runaway train scenarios, what do you think the person on the railway bridge should do and why?

2 Why did Philippa Foot create the runaway train thought experiment?

3 Do you think pulling the lever is less wrong than the doctor or judge killing one person? Explain why.

4 What are some of the ethical issues facing designers of driverless cars?

5 'The only thing to consider when making ethical decisions is the number of people affected.' Discuss.

Unit 2: Ethics
What is the banality of evil?

What causes ordinary people to do appalling things?

The Holocaust

From 1933 to 1945, Germany was ruled by a political party called the Nazis. Their leader Adolf Hitler hated Jews and wanted to eliminate them. During his rule, Jewish men, women and children were forced onto trains that transported them to concentration camps. Here, they were either forced to work in horrendous conditions, or sent straight to gas chambers where they were killed and their bodies burned. Between 1933 and 1945, six million of the nine million Jews living in Europe were killed. This is known as the **Holocaust**.

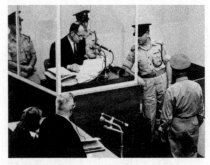

Adolf Eichmann in the Jerusalem courtroom where he was tried for war crimes in 1961.

How was Adolf Eichmann involved?

Adolf Eichmann was a senior Nazi. His job was to organise the most efficient way of transporting Jews from their homes to concentration camps. While he didn't kill any Jews with his own hands, he played a key role in the process that led to the death of millions. After the Holocaust, Eichmann fled to Argentina, where he lived secretly for a number of years, before being captured by the Israeli secret police and put on trial in Jerusalem in 1961.

Why did Hannah Arendt attend Eichmann's trial?

Hannah Arendt was a German Jewish philosopher born in 1906. She had fled the Nazis at a young age and moved to the USA. She wanted to attend the trial of Eichmann in order to understand what sort of man would do such evil and why. Arendt wrote about the trial while working as a journalist for *The New Yorker* magazine, and later wrote a whole book about it called *Eichmann in Jerusalem*.

A monster or unthinking clown?

The people prosecuting Eichmann portrayed him as a bloodthirsty, sadistic monster, and most historical writings about him agree. However, Hannah Arendt had a different view. She thought that the really frightening thing about Eichmann was that he appeared quite normal. She saw him as an ordinary man busy carrying out orders from those above him, without thinking for himself. In a society where the killing of Jews was an everyday occurrence, Eichmann had no reason to question whether what he was doing was wrong. From a young age, people in Nazi Germany were taught that Jews were inferior, with Hitler blaming them for everything wrong with Germany. Eichmann's view of normality had been so warped by Nazi ideas that his actions seemed normal to him. He did not have to break any laws, and he did not have to go against his conscience. In fact, both his conscience and the laws of Germany confirmed to him that he was doing what was right.

Hannah Arendt (1906–1975) reported on Eichmann's trial.

Throughout his trial, Eichmann claimed that he was innocent. He saw himself as an administrator, a train-timetable creator following commands and obeying the law, not a mass murderer responsible for one of the greatest acts of evil ever carried out. It is unclear whether Eichmann really believed this or whether he just thought it was his best defence. However, the court was not convinced and Eichmann was hanged in 1962.

Arendt thought that Eichmann's actions were undoubtedly evil and deserving of punishment. However, his intentions were not evil, and this made it hard for her to despise him as a person. He did not have deep-rooted evil desires or a hatred of Jews; he was simply an ordinary, unimaginative man who, by not thinking enough about what he was doing, had taken a leading role in a horrendous atrocity. Arendt described Eichmann as a shallow, foolish clown, but she did not think he was a bloodthirsty monster. During his trial, Eichmann himself claimed the mere sight of blood frightened him.

> 66 I was struck by a manifest shallowness in the doer that made it impossible to trace the incontestable evil of his deeds to any deeper level of roots or motives. 99
>
> Hannah Arendt

Was Arendt right about evil?

The experience of watching Eichmann's trial led Arendt to think more generally about why evil happens. She used the phrase '**the banality of evil**' to describe how evil can result from ordinary, thoughtless behaviour such as Eichmann's. The word 'banal' means normal, common, dull and unoriginal. Arendt's view of evil was radical. In literature, films and history, evil people are usually portrayed as sinister, sadistic villains with bad intentions. However, Arendt believed evil could be far harder to notice because it can be shallow or surface level, without motive. She wrote that evil 'spread like a fungus over the surface'.

Furthermore, Arendt suggested that if Eichmann had not lived in Nazi Germany, he would not have committed evil; his actions were a result of him doing what was socially acceptable and therefore felt morally acceptable. In the same situation, an otherwise good person would have perhaps done the same. Arendt's view suggests that as long as our morality is socially acceptable, we will not question it. Our ideas of right and wrong are wholly shaped by our surroundings.

This challenges the view that humans have an inbuilt, natural sense of right and wrong. Arendt's view of evil as thoughtless rather than bloodthirsty is rejected by many, and even she did not think that everything that happened in Nazi Germany could be explained as 'the banality of evil'. However, Arendt did think that much evil in the world is banal. In order to prevent such evil from happening again, she thought people must take care not to blindly follow orders and instead, think, speak and act for themselves.

Think

Do you think there are examples of the banality of evil in the world today?

Key vocabulary

the banality of evil A phrase used by Hannah Arendt to describe how evil can result from ordinary, thoughtless behaviour

Holocaust The killing of six million Jews by the Nazis in Germany between 1933 and 1945

Check your understanding

1. Who was Adolf Eichmann and what did he do?
2. How did Arendt explain Eichmann's actions?
3. What did Hannah Arendt mean by 'the banality of evil'?
4. What did Arendt think people should do in order to avoid such evil happening again?
5. 'Arendt's views on both Eichmann and why evil happens are unconvincing.' Discuss.

Are we more than mere matter?

What makes us human? Are we simply a collection of our bodily parts, or is there more to us and why does this question have big implications?

Dualism and materialism

For over 2500 years, philosophers have wondered what it is that makes us human. We can see that people have a brain, heart, lungs, kidneys and so on, but is this all we are? Are we simply physical matter, or do we also have some other kind of invisible, non-physical part to us, such as a mind or soul?

The belief that humans have both a body and another separate, invisible part such as a mind or soul is called **dualism**. The opposite of dualism is **materialism**. Materialists believe that the only thing that exists is physical matter and the movement, or physical reactions, of this matter. This means that there is no part of humans that is not physical. Our consciousness or mind is not a separate, invisible part of us; it is just a word used to describe what our matter does. Our thoughts, memories, opinions and emotions are the movement, activity or physical reactions of our physical matter or body. This view has big consequences. If materialists are right, then when we die, our matter simply decays and there is no separate part of us that lives on.

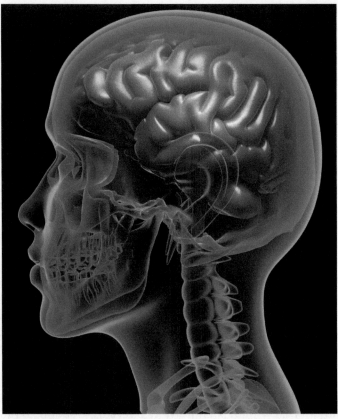

Materialists and dualists disagree about the nature of human consciousness.

Do we talk about ourselves accurately?

If someone said, 'Mr Smith has been found' we would think Mr Smith had been missing but is now safe. However, if someone said, 'Mr Smith's body has been found', we would think Mr Smith is dead. The way that we talk about this suggests that our body is not the only part of us. However, materialists claim that we think and talk about ourselves inaccurately because Mr Smith and Mr Smith's body are the same thing. Mr Smith is nothing more than his body and its movements; there is no other part to him. When we say, 'I have a body', we make it sound as if there is some part to us – some 'I' – that directs our body. For a materialist, a more accurate statement is 'I am a body', because we are nothing more than matter and its movements.

Are we like programmed machines?

When a GPS device gives us directions, it does not actually understand where it is or what it is asking us to do; it does not know the meaning of its instructions. The GPS device is simply a programmed machine with no understanding or awareness of what it is doing. We humans think that we are different from this, but if we are simply matter then, perhaps our brains are like programmed computers and we are not so different after all. This might mean that we do not have free will. This is because there is no separate consciousness making choices about what our physical matter does; there is just undirected movement of matter. Furthermore, if we are just physical matter, then, in theory, we should be able to create something identical to a human in the future. As you will see in the next chapter, this raises many ethical questions.

Is the human mind different from a programmed machine?

The ghost in the machine

The 20th-century English philosopher Gilbert Ryle famously mocked dualism, describing it as believing there is a 'ghost in the machine'.

Just as we do not think there is an invisible force inside a machine operating it or telling it what to do, there is no invisible force inside us, according to Ryle.

Gilbert Ryle (1900–1976)

If we are just matter, is ethics still possible?

Some people would argue that if we are nothing more than physical matter, then there is nothing to make the life of a human more valuable than any other creature or thing that exists. All things that exist are just different arrangements of material, and so there is no reason to value one arrangement above another. Some people also argue that materialism means there is no right or wrong. For something to be right or wrong, immaterial things such as morality, meaning and truth must exist, but if all that exists is physical matter and the movements of matter, then these things do not exist. Like all ideas, they are just the movement or activity of the physical matter that we call our brain.

Key vocabulary

dualism The belief that humans have both a body and another separate, immaterial part, such as a mind or soul

materialism The belief that the only thing that exists is physical matter and the movement of this matter

Check your understanding

1. What is the difference between dualism and materialism?
2. Why might a materialist say that we speak about ourselves inaccurately?
3. Explain why someone might argue that materialism has big consequences for belief in life after death and free will.
4. What did Gilbert Ryle mean when he said there is no 'ghost in the machine'?
5. Explain why someone might argue that materialism has big consequences for ethics.

Unit 2: Ethics
How ethical is artificial intelligence?

Do computers think? What is artificial intelligence and will it improve our lives?

Alan Turing (1912–1954)

The Turing test

In 1950, a computer scientist called **Alan Turing** designed a test to see if computers can think. Turing argued that when we judge a human's intelligence, we base it on what they say and do. We do not base our judgement on what is happening inside a person's brain. Therefore, we should judge computers in the same way. Turing thought that if people typing instant messages were unable to tell whether the responses to what they wrote were coming from a computer or a human, the computer should be thought of as intelligent and able to think. This is known as the **Turing test**. No computer has ever consistently passed the Turing test.

The Chinese room thought experiment

In 1980, the American philosopher, **John Searle**, created an imaginary scenario to try to prove that Turing was wrong. He imagined an English-speaking person in a room containing a book that matches symbols with other symbols. From outside the room, people post pieces of card with symbols on through the letterbox. The person inside the room then finds the symbols in their book and posts the matching ones back through the letterbox. The people outside the room are convinced that the person inside the room can speak Chinese because all of the symbols they have been sending and receiving are Chinese words.

However, the person inside the room has no awareness that they are communicating in Chinese. They have no understanding of what the symbols/words mean and cannot make any sense of what they are doing. Searle argued that computers are like the person in the room. Their actions do not mean they are intelligent or can think; they are simply programmed to match and move around symbols.

John Searle created a thought experiment to argue that the Turing test does not show computers can think.

Would artificial intelligence improve life?

Artificial intelligence (AI) is a term used to describe computers that can carry out tasks normally done by humans. Examples include cars that can park themselves or cameras that can adjust to the amount of light. Currently, we have only created 'narrow' AI, meaning AI that carries out specific tasks. However, philosophers speculate about what could and should happen if it becomes possible to create an artificial general intelligence (AGI) that is independently able to do all that humans can.

It is possible that in the future, AI could remove the need for people to do repetitive, boring work, freeing humans to do more interesting things. However, AI could also cause humans to become less skilled. For example, would we want to create robots that can create better music, art and literature than us? Would doing these things feel pointless if we could never do them as well as a robot? Would human life be better if we no longer did these things?

Furthermore, in jobs that require decision-making, replacing humans with AI could lead to discrimination. For example, if an AI robot decides who should be given a job, a place at university, or a prison sentence, there is a danger that it could unintentionally be programmed with the prejudices of its designers.

Should we create a superintelligence?

Some philosophers also think we need to consider what to do if it becomes possible to create an **artificial superintelligence**. This is a term used to describe an independent AI that has even greater intelligence and capabilities than humans in all things and can keep improving itself.

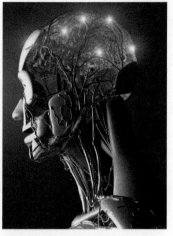

People disagree about whether the advantages of artificial intelligence outweigh the risks.

Humans are not the dominant species on the planet because we are the fastest or strongest. It is mainly because our intelligence enables us to outmanoeuvre and control other species with cages, weapons and behaviour training. However, some people worry that if we create a superintelligence, we would lose this advantage. Machines with superintelligence could potentially keep increasing their intelligence and capabilities until they are way beyond those of humans, leading to humans becoming dominated.

A superintelligence could be able to carry out research leading to developments in all areas of human life, such as science, technology or ethics. Humans might never need to invent anything again. However, if the superintelligence were to turn against us, we could be destroyed. We cannot assume that we would just be able to switch off the machines because more intelligent machines could be aware of this danger and able to defend themselves. We would have lost control.

Furthermore, if the superintelligence could think, feel and act, should it not have the same legal rights and legal responsibilities as a person? Would it be murder to destroy it? Technologists agree that if it becomes possible to create a superintelligence, it will be vital to try to ensure that it is programmed in a way that will stop it ever turning against humans either accidentally or on purpose.

> ### Key vocabulary
>
> **artificial intelligence (AI)** Computer systems that are able to carry out tasks normally done by humans
>
> **artificial superintelligence** The name given to a possible future invention that is more intelligent than humans and can outperform us in everything
>
> **Turing test** A test created by Alan Turing to try and show if a computer can think

Check your understanding

1. What is the Turing test?
2. Using the example of the Chinese room thought experiment, explain why Searle disagreed with Turing.
3. Why do people think that AI could both improve and worsen life for humans?
4. What is meant by artificial 'superintelligence' and why does it concern some people?
5. 'The potential benefits of developing artificial intelligence outweigh the risks'. Discuss.

Unit 2: Ethics
Are animals as important as humans?

Why does Peter Singer compare bad treatment of animals to racism and sexism?

Peter Singer

One of the most famous living philosophers is an Australian named **Peter Singer**. Singer is a utilitarian, meaning he thinks that in every situation, the right action is the one that causes the greatest happiness to the greatest number, whereas wrong actions are those that cause pain to others. Singer argues that if this is the case, then we should think not only about *humans* when deciding how to act; *animals* also feel pain, and so it does not make sense to ignore the impact of our actions on them. Every living creature's happiness and suffering should be equal.

Speciesism

Singer popularised the word '**speciesism**' to describe prejudice or discrimination towards animals. He argues that just as racism and sexism are a rejection of the idea that all races or genders are equal, speciesism is a rejection of the idea that all species are equal. It occurs when people think and act as if they are more important than other species, for example killing an animal for its fur or using an animal to entertain humans regardless of the stress caused to the animal. Singer hopes that in the future, we will view speciesism in the same way that we view racism and sexism today.

Singer argues that many modern methods of farming are also examples of speciesism. For example, to provide meat and eggs in the cheapest way, some chickens spend their lives in cramped conditions in factory farms where they have a poor quality of life. Even where animals are free to roam around, the way that they are killed can cause them stress and pain. Singer thinks that all humans should be vegetarian because we do not need to eat meat to survive.

Singer is also opposed to using animals for research that will only help humans, for example medical research or cosmetic testing on animals. He suggests that unless we would be willing to do an experiment on a human with brain damage, we should not perform it on an animal with a similar amount of awareness. Singer argues that if an action would cause more pain or harm to an animal than it would to a human, then it should always be done to the human. This is because the thing that makes an action wrong is the amount of pain that is caused, not which species suffers.

Peter Singer (b.1946)

> 66 Racists violate the principle of equality by giving greater weight to the interests of members of their own race when there is a clash between their interests and the interests of those of another race. Sexists violate the principle of equality by favouring the interests of their own sex. Similarly, speciesists allow the interests of their own species to override the greater interests of members of other species. The pattern is identical in each case. 99
> Peter Singer, *Animal Liberation* (1975)

Chickens on a factory farm

Is Singer right?

Some would argue that comparing animal treatment to sexism or racism is inappropriate because there are no differences between sexes or races that justify different treatment. However, there *are* significant differences between humans and animals. For example, humans are more self-aware and have the ability to reason and act in a moral way. When a lion or fox kills another animal, we would not call it a murderer or think it should be punished, because we do not expect the same behaviour of animals as we do of humans; we accept that animals survive by killing and eating other living things. Therefore, some would argue, if animals do not have the same responsibilities as us (for example, not to take another life), then they should not have the same rights. It also seems unreasonable to expect humans to act in a different way from all other animals (by treating all species equally) in order to respect imaginary animal 'rights' that we have created.

Fox hunting, fishing, shooting birds, zoos and circuses could all be seen as examples of speciesism.

Some people also argue that to compare the way we treat animals to racist and sexist behaviour is an insult to those who suffer from racism and sexism. Racism and sexism are challenged by people who face discrimination campaigning for others to respect their rights as human beings, such as the right to equal treatment. Racism and sexism are violations of human rights, but speciesism is not because other species are not human. The idea that all species are equal could therefore be seen as devaluing the struggles of anti-racism and anti-sexism campaigners.

Most Christians would argue that only humans have a soul, and this gives their life more value than animal life. In Genesis, it teaches that God made humans 'in his image', meaning they resemble him in some way and God also puts Adam in charge of all other creatures. The Bible does not forbid eating meat and, while Christians would try to avoid causing unnecessary pain to animals, most would argue that medical research is acceptable if it might improve the health of humans.

Abolitionists argued that slaves should be given respect and seen as equal because of the fact that they too were human.

Key vocabulary

speciesism A term popularised by Peter Singer to describe prejudice or discrimination towards animals

Check your understanding

1 Why does Singer think that we should consider not only humans when deciding how to act?

2 Using examples, explain what Singer means by 'speciesism'.

3 Why might people argue that humans should have more rights than animals?

4 Explain why some people reject the comparison of speciesism with racism and sexism.

5 'Humans are more important than animals.' Discuss.

Unit 2: Ethics
Knowledge organiser

Key vocabulary

absolutism The view that certain actions are inherently good or bad

altruism Selfless actions done without thought or expectation of a reward

artificial intelligence (AI) Computer systems that are able to carry out tasks normally done by humans

artificial superintelligence The name given to a possible future invention that is more intelligent than humans and can outperform us in everything

the banality of evil A phrase used by Hannah Arendt to describe how evil can result from ordinary, thoughtless behaviour

dualism The belief that humans have both a body and another separate, immaterial part, such as a mind or soul

ethics The philosophical study of right and wrong

hedonic calculus Jeremy Bentham's way of calculating which actions are right and wrong

Holocaust The killing of six million Jews by the Nazis in Germany between 1933 and 1945

materialism The belief that the only thing that exists is physical matter and the movement of this matter

morality Ideas or principles about what is right and wrong

relativism The view that whether an action is good or bad depends on the situation

speciesism A term popularised by Peter Singer to describe prejudice or discrimination towards animals

thought experiment A mental test in which people think through consequences of different actions, often in scenarios that can't be tested out in real life

Turing test A test created by Alan Turing to try and show if a computer can think

utilitarianism The theory that the best action in any situation is the one which creates the greatest amount of good for the greatest number

the will to power A term used by Nietzsche to describe a natural human desire for strength and power

Key people

Hannah Arendt 20th-century German philosopher who attended the trial of Adolf Eichmann in 1961 and wrote about 'the banality of evil'

Jeremy Bentham 18th-century English philosopher, regarded as the founder of utilitarianism, who argued that pleasure and pain are the same as good and bad

Philippa Foot 20th-century English philosopher who designed the runaway train thought experiment in 1967

John Locke 17th-century English philosopher who argued that when we are born, our mind is like a blank slate (*tabula rasa*)

John Stuart Mill 19th-century English philosopher who developed utilitarianism by arguing that the quality of pleasure or pain produced by an action is more important than the quantity

Friedrich Nietzsche 19th-century German atheist who expressed his belief that humans no longer needed the idea of God by saying 'God is dead and we have killed him'

Robert Nozick 20th-century American philosopher who used the example of an imaginary 'experience machine' to show that humans value more than simply pleasure

John Searle 20th-century American philosopher who used the example of the Chinese thought experiment to argue against Alan Turing's claim that computers can think

Peter Singer 20th-century Australian philosopher and utilitarian who popularised the word 'speciesism', which describes prejudice and discrimination against animals

Alan Turing 20th-century English computer scientist and philosopher who designed the Turing test to show whether a computer can think

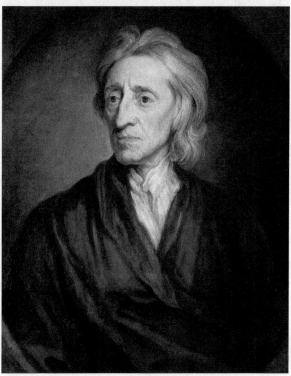

Unit 2: Ethics
End of unit quiz

1. What word is used to describe a person's ideas about right and wrong?

2. In which area of philosophy are right and wrong studied?

3. Which 17th-century English philosopher thought that when we are born, our minds are like blank slates?

4. What word is used to describe selfless actions done without thought or expectation of reward?

5. What does it mean if someone is an absolutist?

6. What does it mean if someone is a relativist?

7. Complete the missing words from the following quote: 'God is ___ and we have ___ him.'

8. Which German atheist wrote this?

9. What did he mean by this quote?

10. What did this philosopher think motivates all humans?

11. What is the name given to atheists who would argue that we should use our natural reason, empathy and respect for others to improve the world?

12. What name is given to the theory that the best action in any situation is the one that creates the greatest amount of good for the greatest number?

13. What is the name given to Jeremy Bentham's way of calculating which action is right?

14. How did Mill's view of utilitarianism differ from Bentham's?

15. What example did Nozick give to argue that goodness is not simply pleasure?

16. Which English philosopher invented the runaway train thought experiment to show that basing ethical decisions on consequences does not work?

17. What is the name given to the killing of six million Jews by Nazi Germany?

18. Whose 1961 trial in Jerusalem was attended by Hannah Arendt?

19. What phrase did Hannah Arendt use to describe thoughtless evil that can be carried out by ordinary people?

20. What is materialism?

21. What is dualism?

22. The 20th-century English philosopher Gilbert Ryle mocked dualism by claiming it is like believing there is a _____ in the _____. What are the missing words?

23. What is the name of the test where a computer tries to trick a person into thinking it is not a computer?

24. Which philosopher argued that this test fails to show computers can think in his Chinese room thought experiment?

25. What term is used to describe computer systems that are able to carry out tasks normally done by humans?

26. What is the name given to a possible future invention that has greater intelligence and capabilities than humans?

27. Give one reason why people might find this possible invention concerning.

28. Which Australian utilitarian philosopher claims that every living creature's happiness should be viewed the same when making ethical decisions?

29. What term did this philosopher use to describe prejudice or discrimination towards animals?

30. Give one reason why someone might disagree with this philosopher's views on animals.

Index

Acknowledgements

Every effort has been made to trace copyright holders and to obtain their permission for the use of copyright material. The publishers will gladly receive any information enabling them to rectify any error or omission at the first opportunity. The publishers wish to thank the following for permission to reproduce copyright material.

Text

p20 Scripture quotations are taken from the Holy Bible, New Living Translation, copyright © 1996, 2004, 2015 by Tyndale House Foundation. Used by permission of Tyndale House Publishers, Inc.; p16 The book cover *The Origin of the Species*, CreateSpace, 2013, illustrated by Jamie Iaconis. Reproduced by permission of Amazon; pp24–25 "Why There Almost Certainly Is No God" by Richard Dawkins, The Huffington Post, 23/10/2006, and Richard Dawkins' speech at the Edinburgh International Science Festival, 15/04/1992. Reproduced with kind permission of Richard Dawkins.

Images

Key: t= top, c = centre, b = bottom, l = left, r = right.

Cover and title page Phonlamai Photo/Shutterstock, pp6–7 IR Stone/Shutterstock, p8 Tim UR/Shutterstock, p9t MatiasDelCarmine/Shutterstock, p9b serato/Shutterstock, p10, 11 Pictorial Press Ltd/Alamy Stock Photo, p12t Granger Historical Picture Archive/Alamy Stock Photo, p12b TijanaM/Shutterstock, p13 Yarygin/Shutterstock, p14l Es5669/Shutterstock, p14r Art Collection/Alamy Stock Photo, p15t Prisma Archivo/Alamy Stock Photo, p15b Mit Kapevski/Shutterstock, p16tr CBW/Alamy Stock Photo, p16br Nicku/Shutterstock, p16l James E. Knopf/Shutterstock, p18l Everett Historical/Shutterstock, p18c GL Archive/Alamy Stock Photo, p18r GL Archive/Alamy Stock Photo, p19 Prisma by Dukas Presseagentur GmbH/Alamy Stock Photo, p20 The Granger Collection/Alamy Stock Photo, p21 Everett Historical/Shutterstock, p22t Kiran Joshi/Shutterstock, p22b Brian A Jackson/Shutterstock, p24t Gary Doak/Alamy Stock Photo, p24c Kathy deWitt/Alamy Stock Photo, p24b dpa picture alliance archive/Alamy Stock Photo, p25 Georgios Kollidas/Shutterstock, p26 Semiotix/Alamy Stock Photo, p27 Jenny Matthews/Alamy Stock Photo, p29 Nicku/Shutterstock, p31 Brian A Jackson/Shutterstock, pp32–33 metamorworks/Shutterstock, p34t Classic Image/Alamy Stock Photo, p34b GL Archive/Alamy Stock Photo, p36t Everett Historical/Shutterstock, p36b Mega Pixel/Shutterstock, p38 Georgios Kollidas/Shutterstock, p39 Luise Berg-Ehlers/Alamy Stock Photo, p40t Nigel Dobbyn/Beehive Illustration, p40b Steve Pyke/Getty Images, p41 metamorworks/Shutterstock, p42t Everett Collection Inc/Alamy Stock Photo, p42b dpa picture alliance/Alamy Stock Photo, p44 Tatiana Shepeleva/Shutterstock, p45t Alexey Boldin/Shutterstock, p45b Art Collection 2/Alamy Stock Photo, p46t Universal Art Archive/Alamy Stock Photo, p46b Nigel Dobbyn/Beehive Illustration, p47 Jose L. Stephens/Shutterstock, p48t Steven May/Alamy Stock Photo, p48b 108MotionBG/Shutterstock, p49t david muscroft/Shutterstock, p49b Everett Historical/Shutterstock, p50 Nigel Dobbyn/Beehive Illustration, p51t dpa picture alliance/Alamy Stock Photo, p51b GL Archive/Alamy Stock Photo, p53 Nigel Dobbyn/Beehive Illustration.